NO LIMITS:

BREAKING THROUGH IN FAITH, FINANCES, AND FREEDOM

A Divine Blueprint to Build Wealth, Walk in Wisdom, and Win in Every Season

BY
LADY NICO BELL

Founder of The No Limits Group | Faith-Driven Visionary

Copyright Page © 2025 Lady Nico Bell.
All rights reserved.

Scripture quotations are taken from the Holy Bible, King James Version (KJV), Public Domain.

Publisher: The No Limits Group Publishing, Rosenberg, Texas
Website: www.breakyourlimits.org
Paperback: 979-8-9937903-0-5
Hardback: 979-8-9937903-1-2
E-book: 979-8-9937903-2-9

ii

Dedication

This book is dedicated to my husband, Steven Bell, my covering, my partner in life, and the man whose quiet strength fuels my boldness. To my children Jasmin, Treveon, Alicia and Jessica—grown, gifted, and walking in your own divine purpose—thank you for teaching me that legacy is not something I leave but something I live.

To my parents, Fred Washington (deceased) and Shirley Davis, who taught me the value of hard work, faith, and perseverance.

To my beloved baby sister, Christeryl Washington-Mouton — your strength, love, and unwavering belief in me have been a constant reminder of God's grace through family. You are a light in every season, and this work carries your name in honor and in love.

And to every woman who ever wondered if she was enough—this is your reminder that you are not only enough; you are chosen, capable, and limitless.

And most of all, to God, my Source. You are the Author of my story and the Architect of my destiny. Every word, every lesson, and every triumph in these pages reflects Your grace.

Table of Contents

Preface:

When God Breaks You to Build You

There comes a moment in every visionary's life when comfort becomes the greatest enemy of calling. When you've mastered the systems, the structure, and the success — yet something inside whispers, *"There's more."*

For years, I lived what many would call a dream life — top producer, respected in my field, and surrounded by opportunity. But what they couldn't see was the silent war between my soul and my schedule. I was producing but not fulfilled. I was achieving but not aligned.

It wasn't until God allowed everything familiar to shift — my health, my relationships, my direction — that I realized: the breaking wasn't punishment. It was preparation.

That's how the **No Limits** movement was born — not from perfection, but from *pressure turned into purpose.* It's more than a brand. It's a call to those who know there's something divine inside them that can no longer be silenced by fear, doubt, or delay.

This book is my love letter to every dreamer who's ever second-guessed their assignment.

To the woman praying for clarity, to the leader juggling faith and finances, and to the visionary ready to stop shrinking and start shining — this is your confirmation.

Inside these pages, I'll share how God dismantled my limits — spiritually, financially, mentally, and professionally — and how you can do the same.

You'll see how faith can rebuild your business, how wellness can renew your energy, how wisdom can expand your wealth, and how your work can glorify God.

It's time to break your limits.
Not tomorrow. Not when it's convenient.
Now.

CHAPTER 1:
The Setup Before the Breakthrough

I used to think success meant control — controlling outcomes, controlling emotions, controlling timing. But God, in His grace, has a way of reminding us that *control and calling can't coexist.*

In one of the busiest seasons of my mortgage career, I had it all — the title, the team, the income. Yet every night I'd lay awake feeling like something sacred was missing. I prayed for peace, but God began giving me *perspective* instead. He showed me that I wasn't just closing loans — I was unlocking legacies. But I couldn't see that while chasing numbers.

Then came the breaking point.

Health challenges hit.
Opportunities dried up.

And the very structure I built my identity around began to shift.

In that space of uncertainty, I learned the most powerful truth of my life: **when God disrupts your plan, it's not rejection — it's redirection.**

He was setting me up for a new assignment — one that wouldn't just make me successful, but *significant*.

During prayer one morning, I heard the Holy Spirit whisper, "You're not here to build a business — you're here to build people."

That's when the vision expanded.
The *No Limits Group* was birthed out of that revelation — a space where faith and financial freedom meet, where women and men alike learn to break mental, emotional, and financial barriers through divine wisdom and practical strategy.

Looking back, every obstacle was a setup for revelation.

Every delay was divine.
Every disappointment was a doorway.

God wasn't breaking me down — He was breaking me open.

Open to new ideas.
Open to deeper intimacy with Him.
Open to opportunities I had prayed for but wasn't yet prepared to handle.

Today, I stand as living proof that you can rebuild from the breaking — stronger, wiser, and aligned.

The same God who redirected me can do the same for you. But first, you must release control, embrace clarity, and trust that His vision for your life is bigger than yours.

This isn't the end of your story — it's the setup before your breakthrough.

And when you finally surrender the need to understand every step, that's when the miraculous begins.

Reflections

- *Where in your life do you feel "in between" — not broken, but not yet built?*
- *What if this is not a setback, but your setup?*
- *Write out what "No Limits" means to you — spiritually, financially, and personally.*

CHAPTER 2:
From Pressure to Purpose

Pressure has a way of revealing what's real.
It exposes the parts of us that look strong but were never truly rooted. It tests our faith, our focus, and our foundation.

For me, pressure came disguised as progress.
The more successful I became, the more I felt the quiet pull of emptiness. On paper, everything looked perfect — beautiful family, strong career, respected reputation. But spiritually, I was running on fumes.

I had built a structure that was celebrated by man but not fully surrendered to God.
And one day, I felt the Holy Spirit whisper, *"What good is building the world's house if you lose your peace in the process?"*

That whisper became a reckoning.

The Breaking That Builds
My breaking season wasn't loud — it was layered.

It looked like fatigue that wouldn't lift, doors that wouldn't open, and prayers that turned into tears. I remember sitting at my desk one day, reviewing files and rate sheets, and thinking, *"This can't be it. I'm meant for more."*

That's when God started pruning.
Not to punish me — but to *position* me.

He stripped away everything that kept me distracted: the constant noise, the busyness that felt productive but wasn't purposeful, the people who celebrated my performance but couldn't handle my process.

I began to learn that pressure is not the enemy — it's the indicator that purpose is near.

Every time I felt overwhelmed, God was preparing a new dimension.
Every closed door was protection from something not aligned with my destiny.

When Purpose Found Me

Purpose didn't arrive as a burning bush — it came as a gentle awakening.

It was in the faces of first-time homebuyers crying at the closing table.
It was in the voice of a single mother saying, *"You helped me believe again."*
It was in the message from a young woman who said, *"I want to do what you do, but I don't know where to start."*

That's when I realized — this wasn't just business. It was ministry.

God had strategically placed me in an industry that impacts one of the most emotional, spiritual, and financial moments in people's lives — homeownership. And He was calling me to redefine what it looks like to serve with excellence, compassion, and anointing.

He reminded me of the Proverbs 31 woman — not just a homemaker, but a *home builder.*
She used her wisdom, work ethic, and discernment to build wealth and legacy. And that's what I was called to do — help families build generational stability, while also helping leaders find their divine blueprint for success.

That's how *No Limits* was born — in the space between exhaustion and revelation.
It wasn't a business plan; it was a divine assignment.

A reminder that **purpose is not found in performance, it's discovered in obedience.**

The Shift: From Success to Significance

The turning point came when I stopped asking, *"What can I do?"*
and started asking, *"Who am I called to serve?"*

Once I made that shift, everything began to align.
Doors opened that I didn't have to force.
Collaborations formed that felt like covenant.
Opportunities began chasing me because I was finally walking in purpose, not pressure.

I learned that the Kingdom way of doing business is not striving — it's stewarding.
When you manage what God gives you with excellence, He multiplies it.
And when you release what's no longer meant to fit, He replaces it with divine order.

Wisdom from the Wait

If you're in a waiting or weary season right now, I want you to remember this:
God does His best work in the dark.
Before there was light, there was preparation.
Before there was visibility, there was vision.

Pressure doesn't destroy you — it *reveals* you.
It extracts your oil. It purifies your motives. It turns your "why me?" into "use me."

So instead of asking God to take away the pressure, ask Him to *show you what it's producing.*

Reflections
- *What areas of your life feel like pressure right now?*
- *How could these areas be divine preparation for something greater?*
- *In what ways is God calling you from* success *to* significance?

Key Takeaway

Your purpose is not waiting for you — it's already inside of you.

The pressure you feel is not punishment; it's activation.

When you surrender to the process, God takes your profession and turns it into purpose.

CHAPTER 3:
The Power of Vision and Prayer

Every empire begins in silence.
Before the blueprint, there's a burden.
Before the business, there's a whisper.
And before *No Limits* became a movement, it began in my prayer room — in those early mornings when the world was still asleep and heaven was wide awake.

Prayer became my *boardroom with God.*
It's where I learned that divine strategy always outperforms human effort.
When I didn't know what to do next in business, He would show me who to become next.

And that changed everything.

Morning Meetings with Heaven

My morning devotions are non-negotiable. They are not a religious routine; they are a leadership meeting with the CEO of my destiny.
Some days it's worship. Some days it's warfare. But every day, it's wisdom.

I start with stillness — before the phone, before the noise, before the to-do list.
In that stillness, I ask one question:
"Father, what would You have me build today?"

Some mornings, He answers with clarity.
Other mornings, He answers with correction.
But always, He answers with love.

He began showing me that vision isn't just about what you see — it's about what He reveals.

When I stopped rushing and started listening, I began hearing Heaven's business plan:
the podcast idea that would reach nations,
the CE class that would educate and empower realtors,
the coaching model that would help others walk in faith, not fear.

It all came through prayer.

Prophetic Planning

I call it **prophetic planning** — the art of inviting the Holy Spirit into your strategic process.
Each month, I set aside a *Vision Day* — just me, my journal, my worship music, and a clear heart.
I review what worked, release what didn't, and realign with what God is saying next.

During one of those sessions, I heard these words so clearly:
"You are not building a business. You are building an ecosystem of transformation."

That revelation became the foundation of **The No Limits Group** — Wealth, Wellness, Wisdom, and Work.
Four pillars. One purpose.
To help others break barriers in every area of their lives.

When I saw that clearly, I realized: the same way I help clients qualify for homes, God helps His children qualify for purpose.
He checks our heart-to-debt ratio.
He examines our faith score.
And when we're ready, He approves the vision.

When Vision Meets Action

Vision without movement is imagination.
Prayer without obedience is procrastination.
At some point, you must do what God told you — even if you don't have all the details.

When God showed me *No Limits*, I didn't have every resource or partner in place.
But I had a *word*.
And a word from God outweighs a world of doubt.

Every project, every podcast, every class — it all began with a seed of obedience planted in prayer.
And each time I acted, provision followed.

I learned that when you move, Heaven moves with you.
When you sow in faith, God multiplies the harvest.
When you trust His timing, you never miss your moment.

The Prayer That Opened My Eyes

One morning, as I was journaling, I prayed:

"God, open my eyes to see the opportunities before me — opportunities to serve, to please You, and to walk boldly in purpose. Don't let me miss divine appointments disguised as daily routines. Let my discernment be sharper than my doubt, and my obedience stronger than my fear."

That prayer became a prophetic declaration over my life.
Because sometimes we're praying for open doors, but God is trying to give us open eyes.

From that day forward, I began to *see differently*.
Opportunities I used to overlook became divine assignments.
People I used to pass by became partners in destiny.
And even challenges became invitations to innovate.

That's when I realized: prayer doesn't just change situations — it changes sight.

Vision in Motion

Now, every plan I build begins with three questions:

1. *Does it align with my assignment?*

2. *Does it serve others or just myself?*

3. *Does it please God?*

If the answer isn't yes to all three, it's not a *No Limits* move — it's a distraction.

Vision is not just about what you want to create — it's about what Heaven wants to release through you.
When you align with that, *everything accelerates.*

Reflections

- *How do you currently invite God into your decision-making process?*

- *What has He been showing you that you haven't acted on yet?*

- *What could change if your prayer life became your business plan?*

Key Takeaway

Prayer is not a pause — it's a power move.
Vision is not sight — it's revelation.
And when you marry the two, you stop chasing opportunities and start attracting divine alignment.

CHAPTER 4:
Faith — The Foundation of Limitless Living

Faith is the invisible currency of the Kingdom.
It's the one investment that never loses value, the one seed that never returns void.

Before *No Limits* became a movement, it was a mustard seed — a small, unseen belief that God could do more with my obedience than I could ever do with my effort.

I've learned that every dream, every business, every miracle must be funded by faith first.

The Moment Faith Became My Framework

There was a season when numbers dictated my peace.
If the pipeline looked strong, I felt confident.
If the deals fell through, I felt defeated.
My faith was tethered to performance instead of promise.

But God began teaching me something radical: *Faith isn't a reaction; it's a rhythm.*

He whispered, "Daughter, you can't build something eternal using temporary evidence."
That revelation shifted everything.

I stopped measuring success by what I could see and started measuring it by what I could *speak*.

When I began to declare what God said instead of what my circumstances showed, Heaven began to respond.
Clients came from unexpected referrals. Partnerships formed without pursuit. Doors opened where walls used to stand.

Because faith will always create what fear tries to cancel.

The Faith – Finance Connection

In business, we track income and expenses.
In the Kingdom, we track *instruction and obedience*.

Faith is Heaven's financial system.
When you obey divine instruction, you activate supernatural provision.

I remember when God told me to sow into someone who was launching their own business — even though it didn't make sense at the time.

That same week, an unexpected opportunity came that tripled the seed.
It was never about the money; it was about alignment.

When you live by faith, you stop chasing resources and start partnering with *Source*.
You understand that **obedience attracts overflow.**

That's why I teach my clients and my team:

"Faith is your first investment. Strategy is your second. Action is your confirmation."

You don't wait for clarity to move; you move, and clarity meets you on the way.

Faith in the Field

As a producing branch manager, faith shows up in my everyday decisions.
When a client's deal looks impossible on paper, faith reminds me: *"With God, nothing shall be impossible."*

When a partner is losing hope, faith gives me words of encouragement that reignite their belief.

Faith allows me to work in excellence without anxiety.
It teaches me that results are my responsibility, but outcomes are God's.

When you lead with faith, people feel it.
Your team starts believing differently.
Your clients sense peace in your presence.
And your brand becomes more than marketing — it becomes *ministry*.

Faith Beyond the Finish Line

Faith doesn't stop when the loan closes, the business grows, or the breakthrough comes.
That's just the beginning.
True faith is tested in transition — when God asks, "Will you trust Me for the *next?*"

Each new level requires a new measure of belief.
Every expansion of *No Limits* — from the podcast to the AI initiatives, to the Wealth & Wellness ecosystem — has demanded a deeper surrender.
Because faith doesn't get easier; it gets bigger.

When you ask God for more territory, He increases your trust capacity before He expands your platform.

Reflections

1. *What areas of your life or business are still being managed by sight instead of faith?*

2. *When was the last time you moved on an instruction that didn't make logical sense — and saw God show up?*

3. *What "faith seed" do you need to plant today — in your time, talent, or treasure?*

Key Takeaway

Faith is the foundation that sustains every other pillar of your life — wealth, wellness, wisdom, and work.
It's not just believing *for* something; it's believing *with* God.
When you build on faith, limits lose their power.

CHAPTER 5:

Wisdom — The Currency of Heaven

Faith opens the door.
But wisdom tells you what to do once you're inside.

In the Kingdom, wisdom is the currency that multiplies miracles.
It's the divine strategy that turns revelation into results.
And it's the reason why some people experience increase while others remain stuck — because **faith gets you access, but wisdom gives you longevity.**

The Prayer That Changed My Life

Years ago, I stopped asking God for money, followers, or fame.
I began asking for what Solomon asked for:

"Lord, give me wisdom — the ability to discern, to lead, to see beyond what's visible."

That one prayer shifted the trajectory of my life and business.
Opportunities that once overwhelmed me became clear assignments.
Relationships that once distracted me began to fall away.
And decisions that used to take days became discernible in seconds.

Because when you use wisdom, confusion loses its grip.

Wisdom in the Marketplace

In the mortgage industry, numbers matter — but *timing* matters more.
And timing is a function of wisdom.

I've learned to never rush what God is still preparing.
Some deals, partnerships, or promotions may look good — but if they
aren't *God-timed*, they can become burdens instead of blessings.

Wisdom gives you the grace to pause before you pounce.
To listen before you leap.
To *build sustainably* rather than emotionally.

It's why every major decision in my business — from choosing partnerships to
launching *No Limits Group* — started with prayer, not pressure.

Divine Strategy vs. Human Hustle

There's a difference between strategy and striving.
Human strategy says, *"I can make this happen."*
Divine strategy says, *"I can't do this without You, Lord."*

Wisdom teaches balance.
It allows you to work diligently without worshiping work.
It reminds you that rest is also a weapon — that peace is part of productivity.

When you walk in wisdom, you start noticing how God orchestrates what hustle
could never manufacture.
You meet the right people at the right time.
You're led to the right markets, opportunities, and conversations.
You stop chasing — and start *flowing*.

Because wisdom knows when to move, when to wait, and when to worship.

Discernment — The Hidden Superpower

Discernment is spiritual intelligence.
It's the voice inside that says, *"This looks good, but it's not God."*
Or, *"This feels small, but it's divine."*

When you're building something big, discernment becomes your security system. It guards your peace, protects your partnerships, and ensures that what you build has Heaven's blueprint, not human fingerprints.

There were seasons where I had to let go of deals that promised fast results — because they didn't align with divine order.
And though it hurt in the moment, later I saw why.
Wisdom was preserving me for something greater.

Wisdom in Wealth

Financial wisdom is stewardship — the discipline of managing increase before it multiplies.
I've learned that God doesn't just bless what you *believe for*; He blesses what you can *manage well*.

That means:

- *Saving with strategy.*

- *Giving with intention.*

- *Investing with discernment.*

- *Planning with patience.*

Wisdom whispers: "Don't chase the bag; manage the blessing."

The same principle that builds wealth also builds wellness, relationships, and influence — stewardship.
When you handle what you have with excellence, Heaven can trust you with more.

Mirror Moments

Wisdom often comes wrapped in correction.
It doesn't always sound like applause; sometimes it sounds like accountability.
It's in those mirror moments — when God gently says, *"This version of you can't go there."*

That's when transformation happens.
That's when character catches up with calling.
That's when *No Limits* leadership is born — the kind that leads with integrity, insight, and inner peace.

Reflections

1. *Where in your life do you need wisdom more than answers?*

2. *What decisions are you rushing that require discernment instead of urgency?*

3. *What is God teaching you about stewardship — in time, money, or influence?*

Key Takeaway

Wisdom is the difference between movement and momentum.
It transforms your hustle into harmony.
It keeps you rooted when others are restless.
And it ensures that your success doesn't outgrow your spiritual maturity.

When faith builds the foundation and wisdom writes the blueprint, *your life becomes architecture Heaven can inhabit.*

CHAPTER 6:
Wealth — Building on Kingdom Principles

Wealth is more than money — it's mastery.

It's the art of managing Heaven's resources on earth.

And when built God's way, wealth doesn't just change your lifestyle; it changes your lineage.

For too long, believers have separated faith from finance, prayer from planning, and purpose from prosperity.

But the truth is: **wealth is worship when it's stewarded with wisdom.**

The Truth About Kingdom Wealth

God never called us to chase money — He called us to *manage multiplication*.

Money is not the mission; it's a messenger. It moves at the speed of your purpose.

When you understand that money follows management, everything shifts.

You stop hustling and start stewarding.

You stop fearing lack and start expecting overflow.

Because Heaven will always finance what aligns with divine vision.

The Four Pillars of Kingdom Wealth

1. Seed

Every harvest begins with a seed.
That seed might be your time, your expertise, your obedience, or your generosity.

I've learned that when God places something in your hand, it's either *seed to sow* or *bread to eat*.
If you confuse the two, you'll consume what was meant to multiply.

"He gives seed to the sower…" (2 Corinthians 9:10)

So, I sow — into people, into projects, into purpose — not because I'm trying to get rich, but because I refuse to live poorly in impact.

2. Stewardship

Stewardship is the discipline of management.
It's knowing where every dollar is going and ensuring it's working for your destiny.

In my personal and business life, I follow what I call the *No Limits Allocation System*:

- **10%** — *Tithe: My covenant with God.*
- **10%** — *Savings: My seed for tomorrow.*
- **20%** — *Growth: Marketing, education, brand expansion.*
- **30%** — *Business Operations: Tools, systems, staff, and excellence.*
- **30%** — *Living: The reward for stewardship done well.*

When you give every dollar a purpose, money becomes a servant — not a stressor.

3. Strategy

Faith without a financial plan is frustration.
Strategy doesn't cancel faith — it confirms it.

I've learned to use tools like **Profit First** to prioritize margin and sustainability.
Every time money flows in, I ask: *"What is this assigned to build?"*

Kingdom wealth demands structure.
Budgeting is not restriction; it's *redirection.*
It ensures you're building legacy, not just lifestyle.

4. Service

The greatest secret of wealth is service.
Money is simply a reward for solving problems.

Every business, every brand, every ministry — its level of impact decides its level of income.
When you help others win, you can't lose.

That's why *No Limits Group* is designed as an *ecosystem of impact* — every pillar (Wealth, Wellness, Wisdom, and Work) exists to serve others while glorifying God.
The result? Multiplication in every direction.

Wealth Without Worry

Money can be a tool or a trap — depending on who's in control.
Wealth built on hustle alone leads to burnout.
But wealth built on Heaven's wisdom leads to freedom.

When you operate by **Kingdom Principles**, you understand that prosperity is not about accumulation; it's about *assignment.*
You don't just ask, *"How much can I make?"* — you ask, *"How much can I manage for God's glory?"*

The Multiplication Mindset

True wealth multiplies because it carries a mission.
Every dollar should have direction, every investment should have intention, and every increase should advance Kingdom purpose.

That's why I teach my team to create **multiple streams of *assignment*** — not just multiple streams of income.
Because every stream should feed a purpose.

For me, those streams include:

- **Mortgage Lending:** *Helping families build generational equity.*

- **Education and Coaching:** *Equipping professionals to lead with faith and wisdom.*

- **AI Innovation:** *Creating sustainable tools that empower others to scale.*

- **Publishing and Media:** *Spreading transformational messages worldwide.*

Each stream flows from one source — *obedience.*

The Spirit of Generosity

Generosity is the heartbeat of abundance.
I give not to impress God, but to imitate Him.
He gave first, and everything I have reflects His trust in me.

When you give with the right heart, wealth stops being transactional and becomes transformational.
Giving opens your spiritual circulation — it keeps your blessings flowing.

Reflections

1. *What are your current "seeds" — and where might God be asking you to sow them?*

2. *Which area of stewardship do you need to strengthen: giving, saving, managing, or multiplying?*

3. *How can your business or career become more service-driven without sacrificing success?*

Key Takeaway

Wealth is not the goal — *stewardship is.*
The fruit of wise stewardship is overflow.
The purpose of overflow is impact.

When you handle Heaven's resources with integrity, you stop chasing money and start commanding it — for Kingdom purpose and generational legacy.

CHAPTER 7:
Wellness — Wholeness Over Hustle

For years, I thought rest was a reward for hard work.
Now I know it's a requirement for divine purpose.

You can't pour from an empty vessel, and you can't carry the weight of destiny if your body and mind are collapsing under pressure.

True success is not just about achieving goals — it's about becoming whole.
Because **wellness is wealth** — and wholeness is what sustains the assignment.

My Wake-Up Call

There came a season when my body started whispering before it began shouting.
Fatigue. Brain fog. Sleepless nights. Weight gain that no diet could fix.

I was showing up for everyone — clients, team, family — but neglecting the one vessel God needed to use: *me*.

The diagnosis list was long: hypothyroidism, high cholesterol, menopause, borderline hypertension, and exhaustion.
And in that moment, I heard the Holy Spirit so clearly:

"You've been trying to heal your schedule, but I want to heal your soul."

That's when I realized — burnout is not just physical. It's spiritual.
It happens when the rhythm of your life moves faster than the rhythm of your grace.

Redefining Wellness

Wellness, for me, became more than a workout plan or meal prep routine.
It became a *covenant of care* — an act of obedience.

I began to see health as stewardship.
My body is the vessel through which my purpose flows.
If I neglect it, I limit what Heaven can release through me.

So, I made a decision:
I would no longer chase *hustle culture*; I would honor *Holy Spirit culture*.
I would build wealth and health at the same pace — sustainably, intentionally, and gracefully.

The No Limits Wellness Framework

Wellness became one of my **four core pillars** because it connects every other part of life.
Here's what that looks like in practice:

1. Spiritual Alignment

Daily prayer and stillness before the day begins.
Scripture, worship, and journaling — the first fuel of focus.
Your spiritual health sets the tone for your mental and physical health.

2. Physical Stewardship

Strength training three days a week.
Cardio for energy and heart health.
Hydration and nourishment that fuel, not deplete.
Supplements to support healing and balance — especially during hormonal shifts.

3. Mental Peace
Protecting your mind from toxic thoughts, comparison, and chaos.
Decluttering not just your space, but your spirit.
Choosing joy and gratitude as daily disciplines.

4. Rest & Recovery
Rest is not weakness — it's wisdom.
I schedule downtime, Sabbaths, and digital fasts.
Because silence is often where strategy is born.

Healing from the Inside Out
Healing isn't always instant — sometimes it's a journey of obedience.
For me, it looked like small, consistent steps:
changing my diet, walking in the mornings, lifting weights even when I didn't
feel strong, and journaling through tears until peace returned.

But the greatest healing came when I stopped seeing wellness as vanity — and
started seeing it as *victory*.

Every time I chose water over stress-snacking, prayer over panic, sleep over
striving — I was declaring war on everything trying to steal my energy and my
purpose.

And I began to notice: as my health improved, so did my hearing.
God's voice became clearer because my vessel was no longer in survival mode.

Wholeness Is Worship
When you take care of yourself, you honor the One who created you.
When you strengthen your body, you're saying, *"God, I'm ready for the weight of what
You're sending."*

Wellness isn't selfish — it's spiritual.
Because an exhausted believer can't be an effective leader.

You can't build empires if your temple is broken.
You can't lead others to peace if you're living in chaos.
So love yourself enough to make wellness a part of your worship.

The No Limits Wellness Declarations
Speak these over yourself daily:

- *My body is a vessel of divine purpose.*

- *I treat my health as holy ground.*

- *I am strong, disciplined, and full of vitality.*

- *I rest without guilt and rise without fear.*

- *I am walking in wellness, wisdom, and supernatural energy.*

Reflections

1. *What area of your wellness — spiritual, physical, or mental — needs your attention most right now?*

2. *How has your health journey mirrored your spiritual growth?*

3. *What would "wholeness over hustle" look like for you this week?*

Key Takeaway

Wholeness is the new wealth.
Healing is the new hustle.
And wellness is the new worship.

When you care for your temple, you position yourself to carry more — more peace, more clarity, more power, and more purpose.

You can't live a *No Limits* life in a limited body — so take care of it like it's your Kingdom assignment.

CHAPTER 8:

Work — Walking in Excellence and Expansion

Work is holy.

It's not just what we do — it's how we worship.

It's the daily opportunity to turn talent into testimony and excellence into evangelism.

In a world obsessed with performance, God calls us to purpose.

To work not from striving, but from strength.

To lead not through pressure, but through presence.

And to remember that true expansion begins within.

Excellence as Worship

Excellence is not perfection — it's stewardship.

It's doing everything you're called to do *as unto the Lord* (Colossians 3:23).

When I walk into my branch, I don't just see desks and deals.

I see destiny.

Each client, each file, each closing — its ministry disguised as mortgage.

I've learned that how I handle the small details determines how Heaven handles my next level.

That means responding with integrity, following up with grace, and leading with clarity — even when no one's watching.

Because excellence doesn't start with an audience; it starts with an attitude.

Building a Culture of Excellence

When I stepped into leadership as a producing branch manager, I decided: Our team would not just close loans — we would *open lives.*

That meant creating a culture rooted in four values:

1. **Honor:** *We honor our clients, partners, and each other.*

2. **Integrity:** *We do what's right, even when it's hard.*

3. **Consistency:** *We show up with the same energy on the hard days as we do on the highlight days.*

4. **Growth:** *We don't fear correction — we welcome development.*

I tell my team often "You don't rise to the level of your potential — you rise to the level of your preparation."

So, we prepare.
We pray.
And we pursue excellence — daily, intentionally, consistently.

Leading with Grace and Grit

Leadership requires both compassion and conviction.
You can't just lead people's performance; you must lead their perspective.

There were seasons when I tried to carry everything myself — production goals, personal goals, people problems.
But leadership taught me a deeper truth:
Grace is the greatest management tool.

Now, I delegate more, I trust more, and I rest more.
I allow others to rise while I mentor from a place of overflow, not overwhelm.
Because when you empower others, you expand effortlessly.

That's why *No Limits Group* is not just a business — it's a movement of empowerment.

We don't just grow numbers; we grow people.

Expansion with Alignment

Expansion without alignment is chaos.

Before I expand in any direction — a new hire, new venture, new territory — I ask three questions:

1. *Does this align with my divine assignment?*

2. *Does this multiply impact or just add noise?*

3. *Will it glorify God or gratify ego?*

Only when the answers point to purpose do I move forward.
That's how I protect my peace while pursuing prosperity.

The world may chase *scale*, but I chase *substance*.
Because expansion that outpaces your capacity is not growth — it's drift.

I've learned to let God determine my pace.
Sometimes He accelerates; other times He pauses.
But He always positions.

Work-Life Harmony, Not Balance

Balance suggests a 50/50 split — as if life and work are opponents.
But harmony? Harmony means they complement each other.

When my wellness is at rhythm, my work flows with grace.
When my prayer life is strong, my productivity follows peace.
When my family feels loved, my business feels lighter.

The secret isn't separating work and life — it's inviting God into both.
That's where *No Limits* leadership lives in the space where spirituality meets strategy.

The Productivity Anointing

There's a difference between being busy and being fruitful.
Busyness drains; fruitfulness multiplies.

I structure my day using what I call **The Committed Success Framework** — not as a checklist, but as a covenant:

- ***Committed Success Calls:*** *Intentional follow-up with clients and partners.*

- ***Committed Outbound Outreach:*** *Creating opportunities, not waiting for them.*

- ***Committed Face-to-Face:*** *Building real relationships, not just digital connections.*

- ***Committed Gratitude:*** *Thank-you cards, small gifts, appreciation moments.*

- ***Committed Excellence:*** *Reviewing systems, improving processes, maintaining discipline.*

Every action becomes worship when done with intention.
Every habit becomes harvest when rooted in obedience.

The Faith-Fueled Work Ethic

Faith doesn't replace effort — it refines it.
It removes anxiety, resets motives, and refocuses results.
I don't work to prove; I work to please.

The more I surrender my day to God, the smoother it flows.
Emails get answered faster.
Opportunities align easier.
And peace is still even in the pressure.

Because excellence without exhaustion is possible — when grace is your strategy.

Reflections

1. *What part of your work currently feels like striving instead of serving?*

2. *How can you infuse more grace and less grind into your daily rhythm?*

3. *What habits can you elevate this week to reflect a spirit of excellence?*

Key Takeaway

Work is not the enemy of worship — it's an extension of it.
When your work is rooted in excellence, fueled by grace, and guided by wisdom, you don't just build success — you build significance.

You become the evidence of what it means to live a *No Limits* life — powerful, purposeful, and perfectly aligned with God's plan.

CHAPTER 9:

Innovation & Impact — Partnering with God in the Digital Era

Innovation is Heaven's invitation to create with God.
It's not about chasing trends — it's about translating revelation into relevance.

When the Holy Spirit breathes on an idea, it becomes innovation.
When you execute that idea with excellence, it becomes impact.
And when you do both consistently, it becomes legacy.

We are living in a time where technology is not just a tool — it's a territory.
And God is raising up Kingdom leaders to *occupy digital space with purpose and power.*

Innovation as Ministry

When God gave me the vision for *No Limits Group*, I saw more than an organization — I saw an ecosystem.
A space where faith, finance, and innovation could coexist.
A movement that would teach people to *break barriers* not only in their belief systems, but in their businesses and brands.

For years, I viewed technology as something separate from ministry.
Now, I see it as a divine multiplier.
Social media, AI, automation — they aren't distractions when used with discernment; they are *distribution systems* for your calling.

Innovation becomes ministry when it's used to expand impact, empower people, and glorify God.

Partnering with God in the Digital Space

When I started exploring artificial intelligence, I didn't see it as competition — I saw it as *collaboration.*
God began showing me that technology, when led by revelation, can accelerate transformation.

That's why I created **No Limits AI Consulting** — to merge spirituality and strategy.
To show faith-driven professionals how to use technology to *build smarter, serve deeper, and scale faster* — without losing authenticity or anointing.

AI became more than automation; it became alignment.
Because when you give God your creativity, He gives you clarity.

The Holy Spirit as Chief Innovation Officer

Every divine download begins with a whisper.
Before I ever write a script, record a video podcast, or design a campaign, I ask:

"Holy Spirit, what are You saying through me right now?"

He gives me *data from Heaven* — strategies that no algorithm could predict.
Ideas that connect, content that converts, and systems that sustain.

That's how *No Limits* content was born — faith-inspired, heart-centered, and algorithm-proof.
It's not about chasing virality; it's about carrying vitality — the breath of God on every word, post, and project.

Impact Through Digital Discipleship

The world is scrolling, searching, and starving for truth.
Every video, caption, and message is an opportunity to minister — to awaken faith in unexpected places.

When someone hears a mortgage video that turns into motivation, or a wellness post that sparks healing, that's impact.

When a realtor hears about faith and finance and starts praying before closing, that's discipleship.

We're no longer limited to pulpits — our platforms *are* our pulpits.
Instagram is the new sanctuary.
Podcast mics are the new microphones of ministry.
Every follower is a soul, and every share is a seed.

The Innovation Blueprint

Here's how I build with both excellence and innovation:

1. ***Revelation First:*** *Before strategy comes surrender — what is God saying about this season?*

2. ***System Second:*** *I document, delegate, and digitize every process.*

3. ***Story Always:*** *I make sure every brand message carry meaning and emotion.*

4. ***Stewardship Forever:*** *I monitor analytics, engagement, and feedback as accountability to growth.*

Innovation is not about replacing God's wisdom — it's about *replicating His order.*
When Heaven's strategy meets human creativity, miracles scale.

Innovation with Integrity

As technology advances, so does temptation — to chase fame, comparison, or manipulation.
But the mark of Kingdom innovation is *integrity.*

I teach my team and clients:

"Innovation without integrity becomes idolatry."

That's why everything under *No Limits* — from podcasts to products to partnerships — passes through one question:
"Does this glorify God and serve people?"

When the answer is yes, the impact speaks for itself.

Reflections

1. *Where is God inviting you to innovate?*

2. *What tool, system, or platform have you been resisting that might multiply your impact?*

3. *How can you use technology to serve purpose, not pressure?*

Key Takeaway

Innovation is the modern language of faith in action.
When you invite God into your creativity, He turns your ideas into instruments of impact.

You are not competing with the culture — you are *commissioned to influence it.*
You are not behind the times — you are building ahead of them.
Because when Heaven inspires innovation, *you don't follow trends — you create them.*

CHAPTER 10:

Mentorship, Multiplication, and Marketplace Ministry

Legacy is not what you leave behind — it's who you leave behind equipped. The true mark of leadership isn't how high you rise; it's how many you lift.

Every seed God gives you is meant to multiply.
Every lesson you've learned is meant to liberate someone else.
And every platform you've been trusted with is a pulpit to teach, train, and transform.

That's the essence of *No Limits*: raising others to walk in the same freedom you fought to find.

Mentorship: From Experience to Empowerment

When I began mentoring other professionals — Realtors, loan officers, women entrepreneurs — I realized mentorship isn't about telling people *what to do*. It's about reminding them *who they are*.

My role as a mentor is to help others identify the gold inside of them that pressure tried to bury.

To help them see that their story still matters, that their past is preparation, and that their potential is limitless.

I teach my mentees three principles:

1. **Clarity creates confidence.** *When you know who you are, confusion loses access.*
2. *Consistency creates credibility. Show up before the applause.*
3. **Character creates capacity.** *The more you grow internally, the more God can trust you externally.*

Mentorship is ministry disguised as conversation.
It's not about competition — it's about cultivation.

Multiplication: The Law of Legacy

In the Kingdom, multiplication is not optional — it's order.
God never called us to maintain; He called us to multiply.

That means every skill, system, and success you've mastered is meant to reproduce itself in others.
Whether it's through teaching, training or team development, your wisdom is a seed that keeps growing long after you've sown it.

That's why I'm intentional about **building leaders, not followers.**
I don't want people to imitate my style — I want them to inherit my strength.
To carry the same faith, fire, and fearlessness that birthed *No Limits.*

I often remind my team:

"If you can only grow when I'm present, I've failed as a leader. But if you can multiply when I'm absent, I've succeeded as a mentor."

Multiplication means empowering others to lead themselves — with integrity, insight, and initiative.

Marketplace Ministry: Where Purpose Meets Profession

For years, I viewed ministry and the marketplace as separate — one sacred, the other secular.
Then God revealed: *The marketplace is the modern mission field.*

Every deal, every meeting, every client conversation is an opportunity to demonstrate the Kingdom. You don't have to quote Scripture to represent Christ; sometimes excellence is your evangelism.

Marketplace ministry is about *bringing divine principles into professional places* — grace in leadership, ethics in business, compassion in communication.
It's when your presence shifts atmospheres and your integrity opens doors that talent alone couldn't.

When you lead with light, people notice.
And when they ask, *"What's different about you?"* — that's your invitation to testify without preaching.

The No Limits Leadership Model

Under the *No Limits Group*, I teach four stages of leadership growth — a model that mirrors both business and biblical principles:

1. **Discovery:** *Recognizing your God-given gifts and purpose.*

2. **Development:** *Cultivating discipline, confidence, and clarity.*

3. **Deployment:** *Operating in your calling with boldness and excellence.*

4. **Duplication:** *Reproducing leaders who lead with the same spirit of excellence and grace.*

The goal is not just success — it's succession.
Each generation of *No Limits* leaders should go further, faster, and freer than the one before.

Raising Kingdom Leaders in a Corporate World

Being a believer in business is not about carrying a Bible into boardrooms; it's about carrying character.
It's about letting the fruit of the Spirit lead — love, patience, kindness, self-control — especially when pressure comes.

Your work becomes your witness.
Your results become your reputation.
And your life becomes a sermon that never has to shout.

That's how you shift culture: quietly, consistently, and unapologetically.
"One conversation, one collaboration, one courageous act at a time." ("Out of Hand Theater is the Best Theater in America")

The Power of Spiritual Legacy

Legacy isn't measured in accolades; it's measured in alignment.
It's not about how many people know your name — it's about how many lives know His because of yours.

Every mentee, client, and connection is part of that legacy.
When they rise, you rise.
When they break limits, your mission continues.

That's how movements are born.
Not from moments of applause, but from moments of obedience.

Reflections

1. *Who in your life is waiting for you to mentor them — even informally?*

2. *What part of your wisdom are you being called to multiply right now?*

3. *How can you use your profession as a platform for ministry this week?*

Key Takeaway

Mentorship multiplies movement.
Marketplace ministry expands the Kingdom.
And legacy begins when you decide to pour instead of preserve.

You were never called to build alone — you were called to reproduce leadership, release wisdom, and raise up others to live with *No Limits.*

CHAPTER 11:
The No Limits Manifesto

There comes a point on every journey when knowledge becomes conviction — when you no longer just believe the message, you *become* it.
This is that moment.

This is where revelation turns into rhythm.
Where everything you've learned — faith, wisdom, wealth, wellness, and work — merges into one unshakable mindset:
I am limitless, because the One who lives within me is limitless.

The Manifesto of a No Limits Leader

I am chosen for more.
I no longer play small, shrink my gifts, or apologize for my greatness.

I build with Heaven's blueprints.
My faith is my foundation, my wisdom is my wealth, and my integrity is my influence.

I lead with grace and grit.
I show up with excellence, even when no one's watching, because I serve an audience of One.

I honor my body, my time, and my peace.
Wellness is not optional; it is worship. I protect my vessel so I can carry vision.

I am a solution in motion.
Where others see problems, I see purpose. I am a divine answer walking the earth.

I sow where I want to grow.
Generosity is my currency. I give freely, knowing that what leaves my hand never leaves my life.

I innovate with integrity.
Technology and creativity are tools, not idols. My ideas are led by revelation, not trends.

I mentor to multiply.
My success is not complete until I help someone else rise. I am building leaders, not followers.

I walk in alignment, not anxiety.
I no longer chase; I attract what aligns with God's assignment for me.

I am the evidence.
My life is proof that obedience produces overflow.

The Daily Declarations

Speak these aloud each morning to activate the *No Limits* mindset:

1. *I wake up full of faith, focused on purpose, and fueled by grace.*

2. *I am guided by wisdom, grounded in peace, and guarded by discernment.*

3. *Everything I touch prospers, because I operate from obedience, not overwhelm.*

4. *I am not waiting for opportunity — I am walking in it.*

5. *I move with excellence, expect favor, and experience expansion daily.*

6. *I am healed, whole, and harmonized — body, mind, and spirit.*

7. *I am surrounded by divine connections and supernatural resources.*

8. *I am aligned with abundance, anchored in truth, and advancing in purpose.*

9. *I am unshakable, unmovable, and unstoppable in my assignment.*

10. *I am No Limits.*

The Spiritual Laws of Limitless Living

1. ***The Law of Faith:*** *Believe it before you see it, and you'll see it because you believed it.*

2. ***The Law of Stewardship:*** *What you manage well, God multiplies.*

3. ***The Law of Seed:*** *Every act of obedience plants the next opportunity.*

4. ***The Law of Wisdom:*** *Revelation without application is stagnation.*

5. ***The Law of Wholeness:*** *You cannot sustain externally what is broken internally.*

6. ***The Law of Honor:*** *What you honor, you attract. What you neglect, you lose.*

7. ***The Law of Expansion:*** *You expand to the level of your faith and discipline.*

These laws are not suggestions — they are strategies for supernatural success.

Reflections

1. *Which declaration resonates most with your current season?*

2. *Where do you still feel limited — and what truth cancels that limitation?*

3. *What daily habit will you commit to living this manifesto in action?*

Key Takeaway

You were never designed to live average — you were designed to live *anointed.*
You carry divine DNA.
You are the evidence that faith still moves mountains, wisdom still builds wealth, and obedience still opens doors.

This is your *No Limits Manifesto.*
Live it.
Speak it.
Be it.

CHAPTER 12:

The Legacy You're Building A Future Without Limits

Legacy isn't something you leave — it's something you live.
It's the echo of your obedience, the ripple of your faith, and the evidence that you trusted God when others settled for safe.

Legacy is when your life continues to speak long after you've stopped talking.
It's when your presence becomes principle — a standard of excellence, grace, and Kingdom leadership.

You don't have to wait until the end of your story to start building legacy.
You build it now — in how you lead, love, and live each day without limits.

The Foundation of a Limitless Legacy

Every chapter of your life builds on the last.
Faith laid your foundation.
Wisdom wrote your blueprints.
Wealth and wellness became your stewardship.
And work refined your excellence.

But legacy — that's the masterpiece.
It's when all four pillars merge into a living testimony of what God can do with a willing vessel.

Legacy is not measured by possessions; it's measured by people.
It's not what you built, but who you became while building it.

That's why *No Limits Group* was never meant to be just an enterprise — it's an ecosystem for empowerment.
A place where faith meets finance, leadership meets love, and purpose produces prosperity.

Generational Vision: The Assignment Beyond You

Legacy means preparing the next generation to carry your revelation further.
It's the reason I pour into my mentees, nurture leaders, and document systems — because what God started through me must continue *through others*.

Every class, podcast, event, and conversation becomes a seed.
And one day, those seeds will sprout into voices, businesses, and ministries I may never see — but Heaven will.

I've learned that legacy is not about being remembered — it's about being *replicated*.
To reproduce Kingdom thinkers.
To raise leaders who build boldly, love deeply, and live intentionally.

"The harvest you don't see is still proof that you sowed."

The Mantle of Multiplication

Every great leader leaves a mantle — a spiritual and strategic blueprint others can build upon.
Your mantle is the weight of your wisdom, the clarity of your calling, and the authority you carry through obedience.

The *No Limits mantle* is not about a name — it's about a movement.
A standard of faith-driven excellence that transcends industries, generations, and geography.
It's the commitment to build with purpose, prosper with integrity, and lead with heart.

And just like Elijah's mantle fell upon Elisha, so will your obedience ignite the next generation of builders, dreamers, and reformers.

Your "yes" becomes their permission.
Your discipline becomes their direction.
Your example becomes their education.

Living Legacy: What It Looks Like

Legacy isn't just what happens when you're gone — it's how you live now.

It looks like:

- Raising children who carry character, not just credentials.

- Leading teams who mirror mission over money.

- Empowering women and men to believe again.

- Leaving systems that sustain when you step aside.

- Walking in wisdom that outlasts applause.

Legacy means your life becomes a map that others can follow to their own breakthrough.
It's not perfection — it's *pattern*.

The Call Forward

The future of *No Limits* is not limited to me — it belongs to everyone who believes.
It belongs to those who see obstacles and still choose opportunity.
To those who dare to dream beyond what's been done.
To those who understand that innovation, integrity, and intimacy with God are not separate — they are sacredly intertwined.

The next phase is about expansion with intention — creating hubs of empowerment, digital discipleship, and generational wealth education worldwide.
A global community of believers, builders, and bold visionaries who live the *No Limits* lifestyle unapologetically.

The movement doesn't end here — it evolves.
And you are part of it.

Reflections

1. *What does legacy mean to you personally — in family, business, and faith?*

2. *What systems or stories will you document to ensure your wisdom multiplies?*

3. *Who can you begin to mentor, equip, or empower today as part of your living legacy?*

Final Declaration

I am a builder of legacy.
My life is the blueprint.
My faith is the foundation.
My impact is eternal.

I live with intention, lead with integrity, and love without limits.
And when my time on this earth is complete, my work will still speak to the world declaring that there are *No Limits* for those who believe.

Endnote Reflections

Heavenly Father, thank You for every reader who has journeyed through these pages. I pray that this book becomes more than inspiration—it becomes impartation. Let each word plant seeds of faith, courage, and divine confidence.

May they rise each day knowing that they are equipped to build wealth with wisdom, to lead with excellence, and to live with power. May their hearts be anchored in peace and their minds illuminated with purpose.

I declare that doors of opportunity open for them, strategies from Heaven are revealed to them, and the works of their hands prosper.

Let their lives reflect Your glory, their businesses advance Your Kingdom, and their stories echo the anthem of *No Limits*.

In Jesus' name, amen.

About the Author
Lady Nico Bell

Lady Nico Bell is the Founder of *The No Limits Group* and a faith-driven visionary dedicated to helping individuals break barriers in life, leadership, and legacy. She has spent over two decades transforming the way people experience financial empowerment—merging biblical wisdom with modern wealth principles.

Through *The No Limits Movement*, Lady Nico equips believers, entrepreneurs, and professionals to build with balance—aligning faith, finances, wellness, and work to create lives of excellence and eternal impact.

A devoted wife, mother, and woman of prayer, she lives by her personal creed:

"Your only limitations are the ones you refuse to break."

Printed in the United States of America.

Join the No Limits Movement

You were never meant to live confined by fear, lack, or limitation.

You were created to live in abundance — in **wisdom**, **wellness**, **wealth**, and **purpose**.

The *No Limits Movement* is more than a community. It's a lifestyle. A divine call to rise above excuses, break generational patterns, and walk boldly in faith toward everything God has destined for you.

Whether you're building your dream home, your business, or your spiritual foundation — this movement is designed to equip you with the knowledge, tools, and empowerment to do it **without limits.**

Here's How to Connect:

Subscribe: BreakYourLimits.org — Get resources, events, and affirmations to keep you inspired.

Listen: Tune into the *No Limits Podcast* on YouTube, Spotify, and Apple Podcasts for real stories and powerful strategies.

Follow:

- Instagram | @LadyNicoBell
- Facebook | The No Limits Group Community
- LinkedIn | Lady Nico Bell
- Work with Me | Explore homeownership, wealth building, and financial empowerment at ladynico@breakyourlimits.org

Your Only Limits Are the Ones You Refuse to Break.

Take the next step.
Join the movement.

Walk in power, purpose, and prosperity — with **No Limits.**

Acknowledgements

To my incredible network of realtors, partners, clients, and colleagues—you are the heartbeat of this mission. Thank you for letting me walk with you through milestones that matter. Together, we are changing what success looks like in our industry.

To my mentors, coaches, and prayer warriors—your wisdom sharpened me, your prayers sustained me, and your accountability stretched me.

To my No Limits Tribe—the dreamers, builders, and believers who carry this vision into every city and every space, thank you for embodying the movement. You are proof that faith, excellence, and unity can change the world.

To my editorial and creative partners, who captured the essence of this message with elegance and excellence, your gifts turned revelation into reality.

Finally, to every reader holding this book, thank you. You are not here by accident. My prayer is that each page awakens something powerful inside you—a remembrance that your only limits are the ones you refuse to break.

No Limits Group Publishing
Rosenberg, Texas

At **No Limits Group**, we believe that every voice has value and every vision deserves visibility. This book is one expression of a greater mission — to help people break barriers, walk in purpose, and lead lives that reflect God's limitless grace.

Our publishing division was created to amplify voices that empower, educate, and elevate. We are committed to producing content that merges faith, leadership, and legacy — inspiring readers to live boldly, build wisely, and believe without limits.

If this book ignites something in you, you are part of the movement.

Welcome to the *No Limits* family.

My Personal Reflections

www.ingramcontent.com/pod-product-compliance
Lightning Source LLC
Chambersburg PA
CBHW051551120626
46551CB00013B/1464